LIVING FAITH

EXPLORING THE ESSENTIALS OF CHRISTIANITY

LEADER'S GUIDE

BakerBooks
Grand Rapids, Michigan

Published by Baker Books
a division of Baker Publishing Group
P.O. Box 6287, Grand Rapids, MI 49516-6287

Printed in the United States of America

ISBN 0-8010-6571-2

Contents

INTRODUCTION

Living Faith: Exploring the Essentials of Christianity is a quick-paced, ten-part introduction to the essentials of Christianity. It is designed for churches to use in adult classes on Sunday mornings, as a midweek Bible study, in small groups and in new-member classes. *Living Faith* is different from other Bible courses in several respects. It goes beyond the Bible to the history of the church, from the first century to the present century. It summarizes important Christian doctrines and beliefs. It compares Christianity with the two other great monotheistic religions, Judaism and Islam; with the two great Eastern religions, Hinduism and Buddhism; with such sects as Mormonism, Jehovah's Witnesses and Christian Science; and with the New Age Movement. Furthermore, it looks at growing our faith through the disciplines of prayer and study, provides answers to common challenges to Christianity and offers some ways to share our faith with others. Lastly, it sets forth biblical guidelines for Christian living and suggests a way for Christians to develop personal habits of godly living.

The *Living Faith* curriculum includes four components.

1. *Living Faith: A Guide to the Christian Life* (128 pages)

Think of *Living Faith: A Guide to the Christian Life* as the participant's guide, which is available separately or as a component of the *Living Faith* kit. The ten chapters of this guide correspond with the ten DVD sessions. To gain the most from the series, participants should read the relevant chapter before viewing the DVD.

2. DVD

The DVD includes ten twenty-five-minute sessions. Each session begins with a monologue from Tom Wright and transitions to a dialogue between Wright and his two conversation partners, Marilyn Sharpe and Joel Quie. Following are brief biographical sketches of Wright, Sharpe and Quie.

Tom Wright is the Anglican bishop of Durham in the Church of England. He is one of the leading Jesus scholars in the world and is also a well-regarded Pauline scholar, having written the commentary on the book of Romans in the prestigious *New Interpreter's Bible*. Wright taught New Testament studies for twenty years at Oxford University, Cambridge University, McGill University and Regent College. He served as dean of Lichfield Cathedral in Staffordshire, England, from 1994 to 1999 and as canon theologian of Westminster Abbey from 1999 to 2003. Wright became the bishop of Durham, one of the five most important bishoprics in England, in July 2003. Wright was named recently by *Christianity Today* as one of the top five theologians in the world; he is also a prolific writer, having written some thirty books, including his widely acclaimed multivolume series titled Christian Origins and the Question of God. The third volume in this series, *The Resurrection of the Son of God* (2003), won the American Theological Booksellers Association's Theologos Award as the best theological book of the year. He also writes on the popular level, a recent example being his multivolume Everyone series of commentaries on the books of the New Testament.

Marilyn Sharpe is the director of Christian parenting and intergenerational ministries at The Youth and Family Institute in Bloomington, Minnesota. Sharpe is a certified family life educator and has been a parent educator for twenty-six years. For more than two decades, she was a confirmation teacher and director at Mount Olivet Lutheran Church in Minneapolis. She has worked with synods, presbyteries, dioceses and congregations and has spoken at Christian retreats, camps, training seminars and leadership events. She has a B.A. from Wellesley College and an M.A. in teaching from Harvard University. She is an adjunct faculty member at Luther Seminary and Concordia University.

Joel Quie has pastored churches in South Bend, Indiana, and Pittsburgh, Pennsylvania. Since 1996, he has been senior pastor of Prairie Lutheran Church in Eden Prairie, Minnesota. Quie has a B.A. in classics from Saint Olaf College, an M.Div. from Luther Seminary and an M.Th. from the University of Notre Dame. Quie chairs and has been active in several professional ministerial organizations and has written several articles.

3. *A Handbook of the Christian Faith* (320 pages)

Also available separately or as a component of the *Living Faith* kit is *A Handbook of the Christian Faith*, the sourcebook for the smaller *Living Faith: A Guide to the Christian Life*. Again, the chapters correspond with the DVD sessions. This book is for participants and leaders who want to go into more depth with the material presented in the guide and on the DVD. Leaders will find the book useful in answering participants' questions.

4. Leader's Guide (16 pages)

This leader's guide will provide you with questions designed to facilitate your group's expression of their initial thoughts about the material as well as their engagement with the material in *Living Faith: A Guide to the Christian Life* and the DVD sessions. Each meeting can be divided into four parts.

1. General Discussion Question

The makers of this series encourage you, if possible, to begin each session with a time of fellowship. Move gradually to the *general discussion question*—a question that allows participants to relate personal life experiences to the theme of the session. If you have a large group, consider breaking it into smaller groups of four to six so everyone has an opportunity to respond to the general discussion question.

2. Living Faith Discussion Question

As with the general discussion question, it is helpful for the *Living Faith discussion question* to be discussed in small groups so that everyone has a chance to speak. This question will provide an opportunity for participants to respond to what they read in *Living Faith: A Guide to the Christian Life*.

3. Video Presentation

The heart, soul and centerpiece of the *Living Faith* curriculum are the *video presentations* that relate to the individual chapters in *Living Faith: A Guide to the Christian Life*. The video segments open with an eight- or nine-minute monologue by Tom Wright, which is followed by fifteen or so minutes of discussion between Tom Wright, Marilyn Sharpe and Joel Quie.

4. Video Discussion Questions

The three *video discussion questions* are designed to facilitate your group's response to the video presentations. These questions come directly from the video. The first question relates to Tom Wright's opening monologue; the other two relate to questions that Marilyn Sharpe and Joel Quie ask during the video sessions. We suggest discussing the video discussion questions as one group so that everyone can benefit from the discussion.

Making It Work

We recognize that the above four-part format is not likely to work for every group. Leaders will need to review the components in this kit and decide on the best way to use the curriculum, given their particular group's size, time constraints and so on. Space will be given after each question in the guide for leaders to make notes and jot down additional questions for discussion.

The Story and Message of the Bible

1. General Discussion Question
For some Christians, the Bible is a strange book, with hard-to-pronounce names and words, a very ancient setting and a faraway, unfamiliar geography. What has been your experience with the Bible?

2. Living Faith Discussion Question
In reading and thinking about the Bible—its canons, structure, formation, message and translations—what are some things you learned that were new to you?

3. Video Discussion Questions
Tom Wright, in his opening monologue, talks about the Bible being "breathed out" by God, which makes the Bible qualitatively different from all other books. How does this idea affect the way you view the Bible?

Joel Quie asks Tom Wright about our covenant relationship with God. If our relationship with God is based on God's covenant with Israel and the new covenant that Jesus instituted at the Last Supper, what influence does this have on the way you view your relationship with God?

Marilyn Sharpe talks about the trustworthiness of the Bible. Do you think the Bible—the biblical story and its claims and promises—is something that we can believe in and trust? Explain.

The Hebrew Scriptures

1. General Discussion Question

In the exodus, Israel experienced the saving presence of God, who led the Israelites safely through the Red Sea. Have you ever had an experience of God's presence in your life? If so, describe your experience.

2. Living Faith Discussion Question

The Old Testament has been called the "roots" of the Christian faith: Jesus was born a Jew, he was raised a Jew and his ministry was primarily to the people of Israel. What are some ways that Jesus' Jewishness affects your view of him?

3. Video Discussion Questions

Tom Wright talks about the sinking of the Titanic, which was caused by ice submerged below the surface, not the iceberg on the surface. He says this is how some Christians see the Old Testament: *submerged* below the surface. Why do you think Christians view the Old Testament this way, and what are the dangers of doing so?

Marilyn Sharpe asks about the importance of Christians knowing the Jewish Scriptures. How important do you think this is?

Joel Quie asks about the early chapters of Genesis—a talking snake, God planting a garden and the long lives of people like Methuselah. What do you think of Tom Wright's idea of reading these passages not as literal, historical accounts of events that actually happened, but as stories that are meant to convey biblical truths?

The World, Life and Ministry of Jesus

1. General Discussion Question

Jesus spent the first thirty or so years of his life in Nazareth, where he grew in "wisdom and stature" (Luke 2:52). In thinking about your own adolescent years, who and what influenced your early life and beliefs the most?

2. Living Faith Discussion Question

At Caesarea Philippi, Jesus asks his disciples, "Who do people say I am?" Peter answers, "You are the Christ" (Mark 8:27–29). How would you answer someone who asked you, "Who is this Jesus person, anyway?"

3. Video Discussion Questions

Tom Wright says Christianity began with the belief that Jesus had risen from the dead—the same Jesus the disciples had known and walked with throughout Galilee. Many today have trouble believing in Jesus' resurrection. Why do you suppose there is such skepticism about the resurrection?

Joel Quie asks about the kingdom of God, which is the central teaching of Jesus in the first three Gospels ("The kingdom of God is like . . ."). What do you understand the term "kingdom of God" to mean?

Marilyn Sharpe asks, "Why did Jesus need to die on the cross, and what does that have to do with me?" How would you answer Marilyn's question, that is, what does Jesus' death mean to you personally and to how you live your life?

The Gospel Testimonies to Jesus

1. General Discussion Question

The Gospel stories are selective stories. Their central message is Jesus' death and resurrection. If you were to summarize your own story, what are some events that you would be sure to include so that others would know you?

2. Living Faith Discussion Question

Which of the Gospels is your favorite and why? If you don't have a favorite, which of the four would you most like to study and why?

3. Video Discussion Questions

Tom Wright says that today there is great disagreement regarding the Gospels' authorship and dating. What difference does it make if we know for certain who wrote the Gospels or when they were written?

Joel Quie asks about the noncanonical gospels. Tom Wright mentions the gospel of Thomas, which he says is really just a collection of sayings, not a "Gospel." Have you ever read the gospel of Thomas or one of the other noncanonical gospels? What was your impression of it?

Marilyn Sharpe asks about helps in reading the Bible. Do you have any suggestions that would help others in the class or group better understand the story and message of the Bible?

Paul and the Outward Movement

1. General Discussion Question
Paul was the church's greatest church-planting missionary. Have you ever wanted to be a missionary? If so, what kind of mission work would you find most appealing?

2. Living Faith Discussion Question
In his first letter to the Corinthians, Paul exhorts the Corinthians about factions within the church, sexual morality, issues of marriage and divorce, sensitivity toward new believers, propriety in worship and other matters. How does this compare to sermons that you have heard recently?

3. Video Discussion Questions
Tom Wright says that according to Paul, when someone believed the gospel message and confessed Jesus as Lord, he or she was justified, meaning that person's sins were forgiven. What word or phrase would you use to describe this reality and why?

Marilyn Sharpe asks about Paul's letter to the Romans, which Wright calls "the greatest letter ever written." Why do you suppose Wright called it this? Do you agree with him?

Joel Quie asks about the term *Lord*, one of the titles Christians applied to Jesus. It was a dangerous title because in the first century, Caesar alone was lord. Do you think the term is subversive today? Why or why not?

A Brief History of Christianity

1. General Discussion Question

What appeals to you about church?

2. Living Faith Discussion Question

The Western church split into Catholic and Protestant in the years following Martin Luther's famous "Ninety-five Theses," which he nailed on the Castle Church door in Wittenberg in 1517. The Protestant church has continued to split and splinter ever since. What do you see as the advantages and disadvantages of Protestantism's widespread denominationalism?

3. Video Discussion Questions

Tom Wright divides the history of the church into three periods: Patristic, Middle Ages and Modern. Do you think this is a helpful way to think about church history? Why or why not?

Marilyn Sharpe says the Western church seems to have lost its vitality and energy; it is at best "lukewarm." Tom Wright agrees. What do you think it will take for the church to regain its vigor and influence?

Joel Quie asks about the Rome-Constantinople schism, which split the church into Roman Catholic and Eastern Orthodox. What contact, if any, have you had with Eastern Orthodox Christians and their beliefs and practices?

Christian Doctrines and Beliefs

1. General Discussion Question
How do you feel when you are in a group of people and the conversation turns to religion? Are you hesitant or eager to share your faith and beliefs?

2. Living Faith Discussion Question
We are called to share our faith. Which of the doctrines or beliefs in chapter 7 do you feel most confident discussing and sharing with others? Which do you feel least comfortable discussing with others?

3. Video Discussion Questions
Tom Wright talks about "the age to come." He says that most Christians think that heaven is a place where we go when we die. The New Testament image, however, is not about our going to heaven, but about heaven coming to earth—a new, transformed earth. How does this teaching square with your view of the life to come? How does it affect your view of life on earth?

Marilyn Sharpe asks about how one comes to faith. Some say we come to faith through our own efforts by inviting Jesus into our lives. Others say that faith is a gift. What do you think of these two views? How did you come to faith?

Joel Quie asks about sin and the reluctance of many to use this term. Tom Wright agrees. He says that we hear a lot about evil but not about sin; yet the two are closely related. What is your understanding of sin? Why do you suppose people are reluctant to use the word?

Other Religions and Beliefs

1. General Discussion Question

You probably have neighbors, friends and co-workers who believe in a god other than the Christian God. Have you ever shared your faith with them, or they with you? If so, what happened?

2. Living Faith Discussion Question

What do you think is the best way to initiate faith conversations with Hindus, Buddhists, Muslims, agnostics and others who have religious views that are different from ours?

3. Video Discussion Questions

Tom Wright talks about Judaism, Islam, Hinduism and Buddhism. Today, Islam is Christianity's greatest competitor. It acknowledges that Jesus was born of a virgin, that he was a great prophet and that he was assumed into heaven when he died, but it denies that he was crucified and resurrected. Have you ever had a conversation with a Muslim about Jesus? If so, what happened? If not, what in this segment do you find helpful in better understanding Islam?

Marilyn Sharpe asks about the two great Eastern religions—Hinduism and Buddhism—and the reasons for their popularity today. Why do you think that people in the West are so fascinated with Eastern religions?

Joel Quie asks about the New Age Movement and its widespread popularity. Do you know any New Age believers or have you ever had a conversation with one? What impression do you think New Age believers have of Christians?

Growing in and Sharing Christ

1. General Discussion Question
What are your prayer practices—time of day when you pray, length of time you spend in prayer, place, format, use of devotionals and so on? If you struggle with prayer, what are the obstacles you face in your prayer life?

2. Living Faith Discussion Question
Which of the many challenges to the Christian faith do you hear most often? When you hear a challenge, how do you respond?

3. Video Discussion Questions
Tom Wright talks about growing in Christ through prayer, reading Scripture, and participating in the sacraments. How have these had an impact on your faith?

Joel Quie asks about unanswered prayer. What do you say to someone who says that God never seems to answer his or her prayers?

Marilyn Sharpe asks about growing in faith through the reading of Scripture. Do you have a routine for reading Scripture? Have any particular books helped you open up the Scriptures? If so, please share them with the class or group.

Living Christianly in the World

1. General Discussion Question

Chapter 10 of *Living Faith: A Guide to the Christian Life* quotes Os Guinness, who said, "The problem with most Christians is not that they are not where they should be; the problem is that they are not what they should be right where they are." What do you think of Guinness's comment?

2. Living Faith Discussion Question

Jesus' command to love one's neighbor is a universal command. As chapter 10 states, this presents a problem: Are we to care for everyone who crosses our path? If not, where do we draw the line?

3. Video Discussion Questions

Tom Wright talks about having the right tools to do a job. Wright says that the Ten Commandments and the Sermon on the Mount are tools to help us live Christianly. How have you used these tools in your Christian walk and witness?

Marilyn Sharpe asks about God's plan for our lives, particularly about God's plan for her life. Do you have a sense of God having a plan or purpose for your life?

Joel Quie asks about issues that Christians disagree about, such as the sanctity of life, pointing out that some Christians are pro-life and others are pro-choice. He asks Tom Wright if the Bible is really so ambiguous that Christians can come down on both sides of this and other divisive issues. What do you think?